COLORING BOOK CRAFTS
COLOR AND STITCH

Vintage Flowers Rag Quilt & Pillow

Vicki Becker

Copyright © 2015 Vicki Becker.

All rights reserved worldwide.

No part of this publication may be replicated, redistributed, or given away in any form or by any means, including scanning, photocopying, or otherwise without the prior written consent of the copyright holder.

You have permission to sell items you personally make from the designs but not for commercial or mass production purposes. You do not, however, have permission to use my photographs to sell your items.

All patterns and designs are sold in good faith. Every effort has been made to ensure that all instructions are accurate and complete.

Vicki

http://coloringbookcrafts.com

First Printing, 2015
ISBN-13: **978-0692579657**
ISBN-10: **0692579656**

Printed in the United States of America

Contents

Contents 3
Inroduction 4
How To Use The Designs 5
Transfer Methods 7
   Light Method 7
   Transfer Pen or Pencil Method 7
Embroidery Basics 9
   Supplies 9
Embroidery Stitches 11
Vintage Flowers Rag Quilt 13
Envelope Pillow Cover 17
The Designs 19
   Conclusion 132

Inroduction

Color your world!

Coloring allows you to explore your creativity and is very relaxing, but you can do so much more than just color on paper! The Coloring Book Craft series will take your love of coloring to a whole new level! You can create beautiful handmade coloring book crafts for yourself or for gift giving.

Vintage Flowers Rag Quilt & Pillow is the first book in this exciting series. This book has 56 floral designs and instructions on how to make a throw size rag quilt and envelope pillow cover. There are also instructions for transferring the designs to fabric, coloring, and embroidery.

Crayon tinted and embroidered designs were very popular in America from the 1920's until the mid-1940's. Iron-on transfers were used, colored with crayons, heat set, and then hand embroidered. Homemakers made household items such as table linens, pillows, dish towels, and quilts.

This coloring activity book will explain how to transfer the coloring book designs onto fabric, color, heat set, and then embroider or highlight the designs with ink. Embroidery is a great way to add a special touch to your coloring projects requiring only a few basic inexpensive tools and materials that you can find in any craft store. All you really need to get started is a needle, floss, embroidery hoop, and fabric. Crafters of all skill levels find embroidery one of the easiest and most addictive ways to personalize everyday objects.

Using this book for craft projects is easy! A link to the designs for you to download in PDF format is at the end of the book. Print out the designs as many times as you wish to use for crafting or just to color. The PDF pages make it easy to resize the designs to fit your project. Use them for sewing, quilting, and embroidery projects or embellish ready-made items such as t-shirts, tote bags, and aprons.

This beautiful book is also perfect for coloring with your choice of pencils, markers, gel pens or crayons. When coloring in the book place a piece of paper behind the page you are coloring to absorb markers or gel pens that may bleed through. Download and use the PDF formatted designs to print on card stock, note cards, or specialty papers. The floral designs create a relaxing artistic experience that anyone can enjoy and once completed are ideal for card making, framing, and gift-giving.

I hope you will enjoy using the designs in this unique coloring crafts book.

Vicki

How To Use The Designs

Fabrics

100% cotton fabrics work the best for crayon tinting. Quilter's cotton, unbleached muslin, or broadcloth is a good choice. Tone on tone fabrics look especially nice when combined with embroidery. Readymade items can include t-shirts, aprons, dish towels, tote bags, and plain pillow covers.

Pre-wash your fabric or item you are coloring

Wash the fabric or item as you normally would but do not use fabric softeners. Iron the fabric or item you will be coloring on. The fabric to be colored should be smooth and free of wrinkles.

Transfer or trace the design onto the fabric

Print out, copy, or trace from the book, the designs you will be using for your project. A PDF link is found at the end of this book to easily print the designs. Reduce or enlarge the design to the size you need for your project. The design should be at least one inch smaller than the fabric or area you plan to color. Transfer the design to fabric using one of the methods explained in the transfer methods section of the book.

Stabilize the fabric

To stabilize the fabric for ease of applying color, it is recommended that the fabric either be backed with contact paper or ironed onto freezer paper before coloring on it. To apply freezer paper to the back of your fabric place the shiny side of the paper down and iron in place.

Coloring

Make sure your fabric is free of threads and lint before starting to color. I run a lint roller over the design area before I begin. Use regular or fabric crayons to color your design. When coloring, work from the top down. Crayons can smudge if you rub your hand over them while coloring. If any crayon flakes appear on your fabric, don't wipe them away, instead gently blow them from the fabric to prevent smudging. In applying crayons, use the method you like best just so the fabric will be completely colored. I like to use a small circular motion. For deep, rich effects, apply the crayon heavily. Rub one color over another for mixtures. A color over white crayon produces a tint.

Heat setting the design

Use white paper towels or plain paper to heat set the design. The iron needs to be set to the hottest temperature that the fabric used can withstand with no steam. Remove the freezer or contact paper from the back of the fabric and place design face up on paper towels or paper to protect your ironing board. Cover the design area with a layer of white paper towels or paper to absorb the excess wax and begin pressing. Change the paper and continue pressing until there is no longer any wax color coming off on the paper. When you are finished, turn the fabric over and steam set the backside of your crayoned design. The colors of the design will be lighter after heat setting. If you are not pleased with the results you can go back and repeat the coloring and heat setting process again.

Ink or embroider the design

To finish your design use micron permanent ink pens or gel rollers for fabric to outline and highlight the design. You can also embroider the design. You will find tips for embroidery in the embroidery section of the book.

Fabric care

When washing your completed item, do not use harsh detergents, wash in cold water and dry on a low heat setting or air dry.

Transfer Methods

Light Method

The method I use most to trace the designs is by using a light box or window. This method is used for light colored fabrics and items that when a light is behind the paper pattern and fabric you can see the lines to trace the design onto the fabric.

When tracing the designs to fabric use masking tape or pins to secure the paper pattern onto the wrong side so it doesn't move. You can then move the fabric around on the light box when tracing. Trace the design using a Pigma Micron pen or any permanent ink pen. I don't use markers because they smudge and spread into the fabric making the lines too thick.

If you don't have a light box you can use things around the house or just use a window. I've used my sliding glass door on a sunny afternoon. I've used a glass coffee table with a light underneath and a glass cutting board held up by cups and a small flat LED flashlight underneath.

You can purchase inexpensive light boxes or even build your own. My husband built me a nice light box from scrap plywood. I had a piece of Plexiglas cut to size at the hardware store and then placed a small fluorescent light strip found at IKEA inside the box. Use a cool light source such as fluorescent or LED.

Transfer Pen or Pencil Method

This method is used for fabrics and items that you can't easily see through when a light source is placed behind it. I use this method for darker color t-shirts, canvas tote bags, aprons, and light weight chambray or denim. To trace the designs you will need a hot-iron transfer pen or pencil. Sulky brand transfer pens come in a variety of colors, including white for use on dark colored fabrics.

Trace the design with the transfer pen or pencil by placing the paper on a light box or window print side down. Trace the design on the back side of the paper pattern. You can also use tracing paper placed on top of the design to trace. If you use this method make sure to make a mirror image of the design first if direction is important as in monograms and lettering.

Pin the design to the fabric and iron the design to your fabric following the directions for the pen or pencils you are using. Cover the design with a piece of plain paper to protect your iron and use the hottest setting usually the cotton setting. Press, then lift the iron and press another area until your design is transferred. Do not rub the iron around on the paper as the design may shift and cause the lines to be blurry. You can check to see if the image has transferred by removing a pin and lifting a corner of the paper.

COLORING BOOK
CRAFTS
COLOR AND STITCH

Embroidery Basics

Hand embroidery has a lot in common with the relaxation qualities of coloring. Embroidery is an art form that has brought pleasure and admiration for centuries. There really can be no mistakes as each creation is your own personal art production. Your selections of yarns, threads, colors and techniques makes each embroidered creation uniquely yours.

Supplies

Embroidery requires only a few basic inexpensive tools and materials that you can find in any craft store. All you really need to get started is a needle, floss, and some fabric but there are a few other items that will come in handy as well.

Embroidery Floss

Embroidery floss comes in many colors and is sold in small bundles or skeins. Floss is made up of six threads or plies twisted together. To embroider measure off and cut twelve to eighteen inches of floss and separate the threads into groups to stitch with. Most embroidery projects are stitched using two or three plies together but you can use up to six.

Embroidery Hoops

Embroidery hoops have two round frames that fit together and tighten with a screw. The frames hold your fabric tightly between them as you stitch. They come in plastic or wood and in many different sizes. You can use different sized hoops for different sized projects, but I've found that a six inch circle is a good one for most projects.

Hooping your fabric will give you a tight, smooth surface to stitch on, and will prevent puckering. To hoop your fabric, first loosen the screw and separate the two parts of the hoop. The section of the embroidery to be worked is place over the smaller of the hoops. The larger hoop is then pressed down over the fabric onto the smaller hoop. The last step is to tighten the screw to hold the work taut.

Needles

There's really no special size or type of needle you have to use for embroidering. All you really need is one with a sharp point and an eye large enough for you to thread easily. You might also want a small pincushion close by so your needles don't get lost.

Fabric Stabilizer

You may want to apply a fabric stabilizer to the back of your project before embroidering to keep the fabric from stretching while you work. Stretchy, flimsy, and loose weave fabrics are much easier to embroider if you first apply a fabric stabilizer to the back. There are many types of fabric stabilizer. Look for a thinner, iron-on stabilizer intended for machine embroidery because it's easier to stitch through.

To apply the stabilizer, cut a piece slightly larger than the entire design. Iron the fabric to remove wrinkles and apply the stabilizer to the back of the fabric, or wrong side, according to the instructions on the package. After you finish embroidering the entire design, you can remove the stabilizer by carefully pulling it from the fabric. Use tweezers to remove any bits of stabilizer that may be caught under the stitches.

Scissors

Keep a pair of small sharp sewing scissors on hand while embroidering. You need them to cut lengths of floss and snip off any leftover floss when you're finished stitching. Embroidery scissors are 4 to 5 inches long and have very sharp points.

Needle Threader

If you are having trouble threading your needle a needle threader makes the job quick and easy.

Embroidery Stitches

Although there are over 300 named embroidery stitches, only a few stitches generally are used for tinted embroidery. The outline stitch or stem stitch is often used, as the name implies to create flower stems or to outline pictures. The straight stitch may be used for highlighting or for parallel short lines as in the fur on a rabbit. The satin stitch or flat stitch is often used for filing in. The French knot is frequently used for dots, as in flower centers or for small eyes as in an animal. The loop stitch or lazy daisy stitch is often used for flower petals or leaves. Any of these stitches, or a combination of them, may go into a single piece to achieve the effects you want.

Stitching the Design

When starting embroidery, make a few small running stitches along the line to be embroidered, and then make one back stitch. No knots should appear on the wrong side of the work. When the thread becomes too short, finish it off as follows: Draw the thread to the wrong side of the work, weave the needle in and out of the stitches of the completed embroidery, then cut the thread close to the work. The wrong side of the work should be as neat as the right side, therefore do not carry the thread from one design area to another.

Outline or Stem Stitch

This stitch is worked from left to right, taking regular, slightly slanting stitches along the line of the design. The thread always emerges on the left side of the previous stitch. This stitch is generally used for flower stems and outlines.

Straight Stitch (also known as Single Satin Stitch)

This is shown as single, spaced stitches worked either in a regular or irregular manner. Sometimes the stitches are of varying size. The stitches should be neither too long nor too loose.

Cross Stitch

Bring the needle through on the lower right line of the cross and insert at the top of the same line, taking a stitch through the fabric to lower left line (A). Continue to the end of the row in this way and on the return journey, complete the other half of the cross (B). It is important that the top strands of all the stitches point in one direction.

Running Stitch

Pass the needle over and under the fabric, making the upper stitches of equal length. Under stitches should also be of equal length, but half the size or less of the upper stitches.

Back Stitch

Bring the thread through on the stitching line, and then take a small backward stitch through the fabric. Bring the needle through again a little in front of the first stitch, take another backward stitch, pushing the needle in at the point where it first came through.

Satin Stitch

Work Straight Stitches across the shape as shown in the diagram. If desired, Running Stitch or Back Stitch may be worked first to form padding underneath, to give a raised effect. Care must be taken to keep a good edge. Do not make the stitches too long, as then they could be pulled out of position.

Long and Short Stitch

This form of Satin Stitch is so named as all the stitches are of varying lengths. It is often used to fill a shape which is too large or too irregular to be covered by Satin Stitch and it also can be used to achieve a shaded effect.

Lazy Daisy Stitch

Bring the thread out at the top of the line and hold down with your left thumb. Insert the needle where it last emerged and bring the point out a short distance away (A). Fasten each loop at the foot with a small stitch (B). This stitch may be worked singly or in groups to form flower petals.

French Knots

Bring the thread out at the required position. Hold the thread down with the left thumb and encircle the thread twice with the needle (1). Still holding the thread firmly, twist the needle back to the starting point and insert it close to where the thread first emerged (2). Pull thread through to the back and secure to finish making the French knot (3).

Vintage Flowers Rag Quilt

Rag quilts are so quick and easy to make that once you learn how to make them; you won't be able to stop! The quilts are made using a quilt-as-you-go method, meaning that each piece of fabric is sandwiched with its batting and backing before the quilt is stitched together. The technique that makes rag quilting unique from other quilting methods is the fraying of exposed seams. This gives rag quilts their characteristic "raggedy" appearance. The download link for the PDF that contains the designs and color photographs is at the end of the book.

Project Specifications

Skill Level: Beginner
Finished Quilt Size: 47.5 X 57 inches
Block Size: 9 ½" X 9 ½"
Number of Blocks: 30

Yardage Requirements

Note: Yardage is based on 45" wide fabric. Quilt batting is based on 90" batting sold by the yard.

Fabric & Batting

1 ½ yds - Unbleached muslin, broadcloth, or quilter's cotton (cream, ivory, or white) for design squares
4 ½ yds – Assorted cotton prints in colors of your choice
7/8 yd - Low loft quilt batting
Fusible embroidery stabilizer (optional)

Supplies & Tools

Water soluble marking pen or pencil
05 (45 mm) Pigma permanent marking pen, Sulky transfer pen, or iron-on pencil
Contact or Freezer paper
Crayons
Embroidery floss (optional)
Straight pins
Sewing thread
Rotary cutter, mat, and quilting ruler
9 ½" and 10 ½" inch square quilt template rulers (optional)
6 ½" and 10 ½" inch angle quilt template rulers (optional)
Sewing machine and walking foot
Iron and ironing board
Fiskars Rag Quilt snips or any sharp scissors
6 inch embroidery hoop (optional)
Light box (optional)

Instructions

Preparing the fabric

1. Wash, dry, and iron all the fabric you will be using for the quilt. Remember not to use fabric softener for the squares that you will be coloring.

Cutting

Note: I use a 9 ½" and a 10 ½" square quilt template ruler and rotary cutter to cut my squares.

1. Cut fifteen 10½" squares from unbleached muslin, broadcloth or quilters cotton for the design blocks.
2. Cut forty-five 10½" squares from the assorted cotton prints for the alternate quilt blocks and backing blocks.
3. Cut thirty 9½" squares from the batting.
4. Cut fifteen 10½" squares from stabilizer (optional)

Preparing the design squares

1. Transfer the designs of your choice to the design squares. Color each square and then heat set. Outline and highlight each design with ink or embroidery. I used 4 plies of embroidery floss to cover the 05 (45 mm) Pigma pen lines. Refer to the book section for transferring the designs, coloring, and embroidery.

Quilting

1. Lay a 10½" cotton print backing square on your ironing board wrong side up. Place a 9 ½" batting square on top, centering it ½" in from each side of the fabric. Place a 10½" cotton print or design square on top right side up, and pin the three layers together to form a quilt sandwich.
2. Mark the quilting lines with a water soluble pen or pencil. For the design blocks draw a diagonal line using the 6½" angle quilting ruler across each corner of the block measuring 2½" in from the edges and ½" in from each side.
3. For the cotton print blocks draw an X across the block ½" inch from each point using the 10½" angle quilting ruler as a guide.
4. With your sewing machine and the walking foot attachment quilt along the stitching lines.

Sewing the quilt together

1. After quilting all your sandwiches, arrange the blocks in five rows of six blocks alternating the design blocks and cotton print blocks.
2. Still using the walking foot attachment, stitch the blocks in each row together using a ½" seam allowance. Make sure you put the BACK SIDE of the quilt TOGETHER when joining the blocks. The seam allowance needs to end up on the FRONT of the quilt.
3. Then stitch each row together using a ½" seam allowance making sure you alternate the design blocks and cotton print blocks.

Note: When sewing the rows together it doesn't matter if you press the seams open or push them to one side because the join is disguised under the fluffiness of the seam allowance and you don't really notice which way the seams are going.

4. Stitch a ½" seam around the entire outside edge of the quilt for a "raggedy" border.

Finishing

1. Using rag quilt snips or a sharp pair of scissors, clip all the seam allowances at approximately ½" intervals. Clip close to the stitching lines, taking care not to cut through them!

2. Finish the quilt by washing in the washing machine to fray the exposed seams. Shake your quilt out to remove loose threads before putting your quilt in the dryer. Remember to wash in cold water with no harsh detergents and dry on a low setting.

Envelope Pillow Cover

Quick and easy! The flower design was enlarged to 190% and the flower wreath to 200%. The download link for the PDF that contains the designs and color photographs is at the end of the book.

Finished pillow size: 16 X 16 inches

Material (for one pillow)

¾ yd medium weight cotton fabric

1- 16" pillow form

Cutting

1. Cut one 16½" square from fabric for pillow front.
2. Cut two 16½" X 12" pieces from fabric for the pillow back.

Sewing

1. To prepare the back take the long outside edge of each back piece and fold over ½" of the fabric. Press this down with your iron. Now fold again by another ½" and press again. Sew this hem down close to the inside edge.
2. Lay the front pillow piece on a flat surface with the wrong side facing down, right side facing up. Align the back pieces on top of the front panel, right sides together. Be sure the hemmed edges of the back pieces face in and the long raw side edges of the back pieces align with the side edges of the front panel. The back pieces will overlap in the center. Pin in place.
3. Sew a ¼" seam around the entire outer edges of the fabric.
4. Clip corners and turn right side out. Use a blunt object such as a crochet hook to push corners out.

The Designs

Scan and print or trace for crafting or print on specialty papers and card stock. The designs can be resized for your crafting projects and printed as many times as you wish for coloring or crafting.

COLORING BOOK
CRAFTS
COLOR AND STITCH

COLORING BOOK
CRAFTS
COLOR AND STITCH

COLORING BOOK
CRAFTS
COLOR AND STITCH

COLORING BOOK
CRAFTS
COLOR AND STITCH

COLORING BOOK
CRAFTS
COLOR AND STITCH

COLORING BOOK
CRAFTS
COLOR AND STITCH

COLORING BOOK
CRAFTS
COLOR AND STITCH

COLORING BOOK
CRAFTS
COLOR AND STITCH

COLORING BOOK
CRAFTS
COLOR AND STITCH

COLORING BOOK
CRAFTS
COLOR AND STITCH

COLORING BOOK
CRAFTS
COLOR AND STITCH

COLORING BOOK
CRAFTS
COLOR AND STITCH

COLORING BOOK CRAFTS
COLOR AND STITCH

COLORING BOOK
CRAFTS
COLOR AND STITCH

87

COLORING BOOK
CRAFTS
COLOR AND STITCH

93

COLORING BOOK
CRAFTS
COLOR AND STITCH

COLORING BOOK
CRAFTS
COLOR AND STITCH

COLORING BOOK
CRAFTS
COLOR AND STITCH

COLORING BOOK CRAFTS
COLOR AND STITCH

COLORING BOOK
CRAFTS
COLOR AND STITCH

COLORING BOOK
CRAFTS
COLOR AND STITCH

COLORING BOOK
CRAFTS
COLOR AND STITCH

113

115

COLORING BOOK
CRAFTS
COLOR AND STITCH

119

COLORING BOOK
CRAFTS
COLOR AND STITCH

COLORING BOOK
CRAFTS
COLOR AND STITCH

COLORING BOOK
CRAFTS
COLOR AND STITCH

Conclusion

Download a copy of the book in PDF format to print the designs as many times as you want in whatever sizes you would like the designs to be. I've also included color pictures of the quilt and pillow. If you have any problems with the download you can email me.

Type the URL below into your internet browser. After the page loads right click the Vintage Flowers link to save the PDF to your computer (save link as).

Download the book here:

http://coloringbookcrafts.com/coloringbookcrafts/?p=18

I hope you enjoyed the coloring designs. Please consider leaving me a review. I value your opinion and would love to hear from you.

You can also visit my facebook fan page to leave a message or comment.

http://www.facebook.com/VickiBeckerAuthor

Visit my author page at Amazon for a list of my other needlework titles!

http://www.amazon.com/-/e/B009ZWK7Q6

Visit my web site for more needlework tips and free patterns!

http://coloringbookcrafts.com

You can email me if you have questions.

vicki@coloringbookcrafts.com

Made in the USA
Coppell, TX
13 May 2021